EMERGENCE OF ME

DISCOVERING MY IDENTITY AND THE COURAGE WITHIN

DENISE C. HERNDON HARVEY

EMERGENCE OF ME

DISCOVERING MY IDENTITY AND THE COURAGE WITHIN

PREFACE

To inspire boldness in a person's walk with the Lord by sharing my story. It was a story that I have longed to write for so very long. It was a story that I was afraid to write and afraid to even unearth in my head. As I continued to grow in Christ, I began to understand just how important it is to understand exactly who we are and what we have been called to do in this life that God has blessed us to live. I hope that it will help the person reading it to look deep inside themselves and never give up and not be afraid. To not give up on the life they desire and believe what God has placed in their heart. To ask, it is as simple as that! Ask, believe, speak, and begin to watch your life change once your mind begins to change. Your change will come with your thoughts and what you then allow to enter your mind and come out of your mouth. We are creative spirits, patterned after God, and just as He spoke the world into existence, we then create our world with the very words that are coming out of our mouths. As each one of us takes a look at the life we are living today, and if what we see with our eyes is not the life we desire or even like, it is not too late to rewind the clock. Our words have now formed our world known as our current life. Our change can begin by guarding our thoughts and what we allow to seep out of our mouth, escaping into the atmosphere and mixing with unbelief. We must come to believe that God not only has us, but He has the best for us, even before our feet hit the ground. If you fall, roll over, get back up, and do it again and again and again. We are enough!

TABLE OF CONTENTS

CHAPTER 1
WILL THE REAL ME PLEASE STAND UP

"Assuredly, I say to you, unless you are converted and become as little children, you will by no means enter the kingdom of heaven. Therefore, whoever humbles himself as this little child is the greatest in the kingdom of heaven."
(Matthew 18:2-4, NKJV)

Looking Back

As a little girl growing up in Pennsylvania, I remember sitting by the window in my room, staring out at the night and staring out at the day. I remember sad times more than I remember the happy times if there were any at all. Can you imagine growing up and not knowing that you are loved? How about not even having the knowledge or understanding that you are special? I longed to have that special kind of love and warmth from a parent. The kind that parents have for their children believing that not only were you -- or I -- wanted but that as a child, I was protected and loved, and that I was a cherished treasure of my parents, regardless of how the world sees me and how the world sees you.

As I continued to look back in my mind seeing this sad little girl staring out into the sky, I remember that I was upset. I was crying. Something must have upset me, and yet I was saying to myself that if no one in the entire world loved me, I knew Jesus loved me. I never really thought about it, but I guess I believed this from that little song we all sang as children. "Jesus loves me this I know, for the Bible tells me so."

Yes, I can still hear it in my head. From this little song that I sang as a child came my knowledge that Jesus is the one that loves me, and I believed it with all of my heart. I remember saying out loud that Jesus loves me, and I believed it. I desperately wanted to be loved.

As a child, like most children, I did not have much knowledge of the Word of God, and I did not have anyone in my life to help give me the necessary understanding of the Bible. When children are young, they may not understand who they were called and created to be, just like today's adults. Yet, they have this innocence. They are born innocent with big dreams placed in their hearts, unchecked and unchartered, unrefined and unchallenged by the world, just waiting to blossom into greatness.

As I continued to look back, I did not recall anyone, even in church, telling me that God loved me. Yet, I still knew in my heart that Jesus loved us so much that he died for us. As a child, I thought, Jesus must have REALLY loved me to want to die for me.

I also remember being scared. I remember not understanding the term "the wrath of God." It sounded scary! Therefore, my childlike understanding told me that God was scary and that I should be afraid, or I would be hurt. Kind of like, if I do wrong, I better hide from God. If He finds out, He is going to be so mad at me. Surely, I could not have been the only person who thought God would strike them down if they got out of line. Hearing scriptures such as these with no one to explain them frightened me. Regardless, I still had Jesus and His love, even if I did not feel that love from anyone else.

My desire or need to feel loved caused me to get up one Sunday morning to a place where I was supposed to be and where I should be wanted – my church. Both my parents grew up in the church, but they never loaded our family up and carried us out to hear and learn of the Lord.

When I finally attended church as a child, the surprising thing is that just me and my sister ventured out to find it by ourselves. No parents were holding our hands, making us sit quietly in service, or smacking our knees to stop fidgeting or chewing gum, or fighting with each other. It was just the two of us that particular Sunday. I even remember walking to this church. It was a Methodist church, and as scared as I was, I was so excited to be attending a church service. This was not just any old church I picked out, but I had remembered my mother saying one day as we drove past that we (my family) belonged to that church. I believe I was around the age of seven or eight years old.

I desperately wanted to belong to something and someone, and I believed I had found it. I set off on my journey that Sunday to find my church home. Once we reached the church and entered in, we found a pew to sit on. I didn't recognize anyone there as I glanced around, trying to figure out what we were supposed to be doing. Of course, I do not remember much of it, but I do remember getting many strange looks, although I didn't see it as strange because I was, in my mind, where I was supposed to be.

In all churches back in the day, visitors were asked to stand up. Oh, it just makes me smile now when I think about how crazy it was. When the announcement was made for all visitors to rise and state their name, I didn't move. I didn't get up. Instead, I sat there, looking around as all the ushers came over and asked me to stand up as a visitor. I told her, and anyone within earshot, that I was not a visitor, that I was a member, too, and belonged there. Of course, I was still clueless.

I received the strangest looks from the congregation around me. However, I thought they were all strange for looking at me in such a way because, after all, I belonged at that church. At my young age, I didn't have a clue about what they were thinking. It's funny now when I look back on that experience. It was very funny but also incredibly sad. Sad because I had to go without a parent or any adult for that matter. It was not because of instruction that I went, but a yearning in my heart to learn more about God. I always felt so alone, even when I wasn't alone.

As a child, I remember doing so much alone, such as walking to the library and hanging out. I would never have let my daughter, son, or even our grandchildren do that, but that is just how life was for me. I did not always feel welcomed, yet I tried too much to act as if I was happy in an attempt to hide what I felt deep inside of me.

One specific time, I remember overhearing a conversation about me from a couple of older relatives concerning my appearance, hair, and clothes. These were things that I did not have a lot of say-so in because of my circumstances. Their comments and judgmental glances stung my heart, reinforcing the thought that, yes, I was right! I'm not enough! That false thinking became a true reality for me.

I believe this is just one instance that occurred in my life as a child that made me want to do better and strive better, but for who and to prove what? God has an everlasting love for His children, and even when in trouble, hurt, and pain, His grace is always waiting for us. He only has love and the best for His children. "Peace I leave with you, My peace I give to you; not as the world gives do I give to you. Let not your heart be troubled, neither let it be afraid" (John 14:27, NKJV).

Starting from the Inside

For many children today, learning can be a struggle. However, all of their struggles do not stem from a lack of understanding. Their struggles may often stem from their environment, home life, and family dynamics that they deal with daily. They are forced to exist in cultures where kids are called names, picked on, and belittled. Unfortunately, these incidents may also take place under the radar of educators. Social media has made vulnerable children an easier target for bullying. I was one of these children, and there were times that I was not treated nicely, like so many others.

My parents held me back in elementary school, and I was told they believed it was for my good. Perhaps the learning issues stemmed from witnessing violence within my community. My parents were informed that it appeared I was not ready to move on since I just sat in class and did not participate; they said I needed a little more time to develop. For the life of me, I do not even remember if it was kindergarten to first grade or first to second grade. Either way, I was a year behind and a year older than the other students in my class.

The Bible declares to "train up a child in the way he should go, and when he is old, he will not depart from it" (Proverbs 22:6, NKJV). Growing up, I do not know whether my parents did or did not understand what the bible said about children and teaching and training a child. Yet, I do believe that they never heard or even understood the Word of God.

Like so many others, my parents did not understand what God's Word declares concerning children and the family. So how would they know and understand what they should or could do to instill this into their children? How could they show their children something different, something special? How can you give to another what you do not have or even care about?

I often would say, how can parents teach their children manners that they do not have. If you don't understand how to treat others, including yourself, how does a child know and understand how to operate on the earth? It is amazing how, even as a child, these thoughts would come to my mind and in my heart. I had no one to help explain these questions to me, yet I desired to know more.

As a little girl, I also remember that something awful occurred in our town. There was some sort of uprising that occurred, and I witnessed this as a child. My memory as a child may not be accurate, but there were things that I have never forgotten. At the same time, I never asked my parents about what took place. Let me explain here what I remembered of what had taken place.

On my way to school, I saw a young Caucasian man on the corner surrounded by other young Black men that I believed were gang members because of the times, but that information I am uncertain of. These boys were hurting the young man. I remember them cutting him in his stomach area and putting something in a bag.

Next, a car drove up the street. They put him inside the car and drove away extremely fast. I remember we then had to walk past these young men. They did not bother us, but I was very afraid. I was told to just look straight ahead. I was confused and so young -- five to six years old. Once I grew older, I understood what had happened.

It was the riots of 1968, which occurred after Dr. Martin Luther King, Jr. was assassinated. As I searched for information, I learned that riots had occurred across the country, mostly in urban Black neighbors, and it happened in mine as well. There were fires along with vandalism and looting. I remember none of this; I was just too young. However, we continue to witness these atrocities happening even today in our communities. Black and brown people are still being killed, still being mistreated, and still suffering injustices in every arena of life. I saw this as a six-year-old little girl, and after all these years, I'm still witnessing it today, as if nothing has ever changed.

All of the hurt and pain, the uncertainty about life. Mothers and fathers afraid for their children, unsure if they will come home each day. The hatred, prejudice, and unfairness that took place then continue to take place now. But it must change; it must all change for the good. Not saying anything and not standing up will not make a change. Again, we all matter!

What was taking place seemed like a moment in time for me, one that I never really remembered or spoke about to anyone, and that includes my parents. I wanted to be a good girl. I was never told I was bad, just as I was never told I was good, smart, worthy, or capable of doing anything that I put my mind to. Still, doing what I was told to do was my way of life. It was the only way I knew it to be. That is what you do when you just want to please your parents and hear the love and praise from them.

Like so many others, I did what I was told to do. That has always been my life. Even as an adult, I have lived a life of obedience, and I desire to please others, but my desire should be for God more than anything. That is what I did not understand.

I wanted to be that ideal student and that ideal child, whatever that is or was. When, and if, I did act out or act bold, it was not the true me. It was me trying to "fit in" somewhere, anywhere. I just needed to belong, just as so many children today.

I did not know or understand who I was. I was always said to be a sweet, nice, and kind person, someone always willing to help. This is how others have always seen me. How do others see you? The picture that you are identified with, is it one that is true, or perhaps one that is hiding behind a mask, so very unsure and lacking understanding? On the surface, it appears that there is nothing wrong, not really. But it goes deeper than just being nice and having the "Christian traits" that we should have and display in our lives.

This person, who was always seen from the outside with the smile on her face, dimples in both cheeks, struggled on the inside and did not even know it. The person that everyone would see did not display confidence. It was definitely not inside me. When I was in school from elementary through my college years, I remember being afraid to speak aloud. I spoke so softly that one time in a college English class that I was asked to read out loud to the class. The crazy thing is that I loved to read and considered reading as my specialty. There was nothing like having a good book, and I never left home without having one to read on the bus or whenever I was alone. Reading on my own was one thing, but reading in front of the class was completely different. I was the only Black student in this class, and knowing that made me feel even more afraid of the judgment that I felt would be thrown my way.

My heart was beating so fast, and I believe that day, I read faster than my heart was beating. I was an exceptionally good reader, yet that day, I read so fast and so quietly that when I finished, the other students in the class were stunned speechless, as I sat there completely satisfied as I finished the task I believed I was asked to do. I thought I did it quite well, except for the fact that I knew the other students nor my professor were able to hear one word I said. Nevertheless, my mannerism told them I was finished, and being finished was all that mattered to me.

How do you think others see you, and should that really matter, or should it even matter to you? The important question is, how do you see yourself? Do you value who you are as the person that God created you to be? That is an important question. Do you see yourself through the eyes of Jesus? You are a child of God. He loves you, and He loves me more than we can ever imagine!

Unfortunately, when we do not understand who we are in Jesus and that our identity should line up with Him, we will continue to feel lost and confused, lacking the understanding of what we should be doing with this life that God has blessed us to live. Our dreams matter! "For My thoughts are not your thoughts, nor are your ways My ways," says the Lord. "For as the heavens are higher than the earth, so are My ways higher than your ways, and My thoughts than your thoughts" (Isaiah 55:8-9, NKJV).

CHAPTER 2
APPROVAL MEANS TOO MUCH

"And let us not grow weary while doing good,
for in due season
we shall reap if we do not lose heart." (Galatians 6:9,
NKJV)

Misguided Perfection

"Therefore, you shall be perfect, just as your Father in heaven is perfect" (Matthew 5:48, NKJV). The perfect Son of God is all perfect! Striving for perfection in my life started at an early age because it was tied into desiring to be accepted by my parents and family, my friends, and even my coworkers. How did I become the person I am today? What makes me tick? What makes you tick?

As I thought about it, I believed from my memories growing up that I was pretty passive in the relationship arena, so I started "really" looking into the meaning of passive. As it pertains to myself in its entirety, I didn't like it very much. However, I could agree with what was said. The descriptive word passive states that it is someone that never desires to upset. It can be a person who always wants to do the right thing and be that friend to all they encounter. They are also a humble person.

There is absolutely nothing wrong with being humble and helping others, desiring to understand all things, and desiring to live a peaceful life. I believe this should be a trait that we all, as believers, strive for. But what about being intimidated by what you believe you lack or the strength in others, which may confuse or scare a person? This can also stem from their life experiences.

They desire peace, and peace may mean standing down instead of standing up in these circumstances, just to get along. Just as an optimist individual looks on the brighter side of life, someone that is passive or quiet spoken has these same positive attributes, loving others just as Jesus loves us all.

My transition to adulthood came with marriage and the military. My husband and I went to high school together, and after he enlisted in the United States Air Force and received his permanent duty assignment, I was blessed, like so many spouses, to join him. It was a huge transition for me. It was a scary and very new lifestyle and shift since I had never been a part of a military community.

Becoming a military wife who moved to the Midwest from the East coast, which then led to relocating to Turkey two years later, was a huge adjustment. Every person associated comes to see just how much comes along with military installation. Even simple things, like going to the grocery store (or commissary, as they call it), became a little more involved.

Our first assignment and my first experience at the commissary was intimidating and confusing. It appeared that everyone was moving in the same direction, up one aisle, down the other. I looked down, and there were arrows on the floor. What would happen if I dare went against the flow of the arrow? Oh, how I wished at that moment that I could be a renegade and do what I desired to do, even if it meant bucking the system. Yet, this was me, so going against the norm was something that I would not do. I would adjust, and adjust is what I did.

Military life involves duty, honor, discipline, and structure. As a military spouse, I came to understand just how disciplined and structured life for an active-duty soldier was. I went out of my way to ensure that we, meaning our children and myself, would not make life harder for my husband because I understood this. There was never a period where I forgot how our actions would affect the active duty member. I saw this firsthand when I worked in one of the squadrons, which held hearings concerning family members that broke the rules and regulations, what the consequences could be.

I wanted to do my part. I wanted to stay connected and stay involved. I made sure that I would attend all military spouse related events orchestrated by my husband's squadron, which may not have always been necessary for me, but because I believed it was not only important but expected as well, as I said, I wanted to do my part. In my mind, I had this high expectation that we needed to strive to be this perfect family, attempting to make the right decisions to receive the best possible outcome. Was I wrong? Perhaps, but I was misguided in believing that there was nothing wrong with striving for perfection. How much better is it to please the Father instead of always trying to please people?

However, the striving that I was aiming at was to please people and gain acceptance. I thought this was what a person had to do. And I know I'm not alone. We all perform for others without even thinking about it. Most humans understand and have that knowledge of which hat to wear for which situation. You can be this one in church with other brothers and sisters in Christ, and then you can perform in this manner at work or with your friends. Homelife is yet another performance when you can let your guard down and just be yourself.

Like every other person, I understood which performance was needed and at which time. The real me was unsure of what to do in every given situation. The real me did not know where to turn or who I could turn to. The real me knew that to get along; I had to pretend to understand, even when I did not. The perfection that I was seeking was not after God, and it was not to pattern myself after our perfect and gracious Father. At this time, I did not know or understand this life principle. What I was seeking was the approval of others. Approval to let me know that I was accepted and enough in their eyes when all that will ever matter is the love and approval of God!

How awesome would it be for us all to understand that only what we do for God matters? This is real approval. It does not come from people who do not care, may not like you, and definitely will never appreciate and celebrate you in the matter that one should. Life lessons are a process we all grow through, some faster than others. "And let us not grow weary while doing good, for in due season we shall reap if we do not lose heart" (Galatians 6:9, NKJV).

Things happen in this world that may make us wonder if this is the end. I remember a very scary time in our life in 1991 during Desert Storm while we were stationed at Incirlik Air Base Turkey. All active-duty personnel had to stay in the country. All family members were evacuated back to the United States. I will never forget standing in a processing line, knowing the war was breaking out not far from Turkey, praying that we would make it out ok. This memory will never leave your mind.

My son and I were on "Chalk 19," which was the number of the flight we were assigned to fly out of Incirlik. How mind blowing is it that to this day, I still remember that entire life changing event, including the number of the plane we were assigned to travel on. Chalk19, was loaded with families, children, and mothers, trying to entertain their children, not knowing what was waiting for us when we would eventually land back in the United States.

Just as leaving a family member during war was scary being sent back to the United States, it was even more during September 11, 2001. My family and I had just relocated back to the United States from Okinawa, Japan. We loved living in Japan, but it was time to go. When 9/11 occurred, I will never forget the fear, the disbelief of what I was watching occur right before my eyes, like everyone else in the world.

Like all military families, watching your loved one leave to go overseas during wartime without any knowledge of where they are going or a way to communicate is beyond fearful. I did my best to maintain some type of normalcy for our children. I did not allow them to watch T.V. (news outlets), yet as military children, they knew exactly what was taking place, and they missed their father very much. Still, I remained calmed and prayed that my husband would be covered in the Blood of Jesus. My peace was that no matter what, he was a child of God. Even in his imperfection, he had a heart for Jesus, had received salvation, and loved God. So many of our servicemen and women left their families and their homes, and some never returned. So many souls were lost during the September 11th attacks. So many souls are lost during all the operations and conflicts that our servicemen and women respond to. There are still so many broken families in need of closure, healing, and great love. "Now faith is the substance of things hoped for, the evidence of things not seen. For by it the elders obtained a good testimony. By faith, we understand that the worlds were framed by the word of God so that the things which are seen were not made of things which are visible" (Hebrews 11:1-3, NKJV).

Healing Through Disappointment and Rejection

"Be anxious for nothing, but in everything by prayer and supplication, with thanksgiving, let your requests be made known to God; and the peace of God, which surpasses all understanding, will guard your hearts and minds through Christ Jesus." (Philippians 4:6-7, NKJV)

Disappointments, as well as rejection, in a well-lived life, cannot be avoided. I desired not to disappoint even though I did like all of us do, time and time again. I learned early to not always share those disappointments, and I cannot say that I knew to take heart of those hard lessons, make a better decision, and do what I knew best to do. Most of the disappointments in my life came from me not taking the chances or missed opportunities.

It also comes with making wrong or faulty decisions. The disappointment rides in on the shoulders of whatever event or circumstance is falling apart. Disappointments hurt even more when it is derived from trusting others, allowing others to enter and get close to your heart, only to then feel the sting of betrayal. Believing someone when they stated they would do what you needed them to do, or perhaps even lied about it, is tough. It is not easy, just as offering up forgiveness, but it is necessary to move on in life. It is necessary for you, the hurt and the broken, to forgive and begin the healing for your life and for your good.

Being disappointed hurts. Having the ability to gather yourself up and try again is tough, and often, it is easier to just give up and move on. Living this life on earth, you will experience disappointments, but the important aspect of any disappointment is not giving up and throwing in the towel. For so very long, I wanted to go back to college. I went to college right after high school, and it was not that it was expected of me to receive a higher education. After all, my parents never went to college. In fact, I only had one cousin that I knew went for sure. Still, when I attended my first year, it was not a great experience for me, especially because I was struggling with my identity and self-esteem. I felt completely lost and alone since I did not have the support in school or at home. I went through the motions each day, attempting to figure it all out, and failed miserably.

In my mind and in my heart, after dropping out of college, I still believed that it was for me to receive a college education, and as time went on, I wanted to accomplish it more and more. This was indeed something that I desired more and more to accomplish. The thought and desire never left me as I continued to grow into an adult, marry, and start a family. There were times overseas that I even attempted to go back to no avail, simply because I did not have a clue why I would be going back and what I desired to do. See, I had not sought God in prayer. If I had, those desires would have been revealed to me. When you seek God, not only are your desires revealed, but they will be what He has for you since He is the one who placed it in you in the first place. "For I know the thoughts that I think toward you, says the Lord, thoughts of peace and not of evil, to give you a future and a hope" (Jeremiah 29:11, NKJV).

Why is it that a person feels the need to be liked or approved by others? I believe this is a human trait that all, if not most, of us have. Again, looking back, I have often asked myself, "Did I allow this belief or decision to control my actions and beliefs about myself? Is it what I believed, or was it the opinions of others?" This is not a lesson that we automatically know. Often, we feed into the decisions and opinions of others without digging deep down inside to discover what we truly believe and desire to accomplish in our lives and the lives of those around us. We should not give other people the power and control over our lives and allow their ill thoughts and opinions to control us; it is not right. This always leads me to question just how much approval of others meant to me. I thought about this question, and it was not so much the fear of being rejected but more of believing that I had to prove myself. Maybe I was just proving myself to myself. After all, how much do other people care anyway? Often, I found myself making sure I annotated an action in case I had to show proof. I even found myself doing this very thing with my husband. In conversation, if I said I did something or would do something, and his answer sounded as if it was questioning,

I provided proof, as if to say, "I told you so." He would then tell me he believed me, or it was ok, but it was not ok in my mind.

My mother must have felt like she was rejected. I knew nothing of the life either of my parents had while growing up. Later in life, I started finding out more and more about her life and why she was the way she was. I loved my mother, and knowing some of her story made me understand just how hurt she must have been growing up.

My mother was not a flashy woman, and she had such a beautiful spirit and smile. When she smiled, I could see it in her eyes. I still love looking at her picture and seeing her smile in her eyes. It is as if my mother was smiling down on the inside. When I think about her life, I'm sure she may have felt rejected by her mother. Her mother left her father, her husband, after having children. She left him, and she left her children alone.

What I can say, for now, is what she did share with me was that after her mother left, the state came in and removed her and her siblings from his care because he was reported by a family member to be an alcoholic trying to take care of his children without his wife.

As far as I know, my mother never saw her mother again. She never talked much about her life growing up. However, when I did bring up family history, she became withdrawn, as if she remembered such an unpleasant time in her life. She said, "You do not know how much it hurt to know that most of the kids you go to school with are your relatives, your cousins, your family, and no one cared to help me and my siblings."

My mother and her sister were sent to live with a relative, while her two brothers were placed in foster care. Rejection is a pain that can hurt. Rejection is a force that, if not dealt with, can wound the soul. Rejection can invite its cohorts to join in, further deepening the hurt and the pain. My mother was still hurting, and not only that, but she was also rejected by a family that should have been there for her and her siblings. She was rejected by a mother she grew up not knowing, who left never to return.

My mother was rejected, and she buried that pain and hurt deep inside of her, carrying it to her grave. When I began to learn of her story and her tribulations as a child, my heart cried out for what she must have felt as a child. What child would not desire their mother, especially after she learned the truth? She kept her hurt buried deep down inside of her. Oh, how I wish she would have had the courage to speak what was deep inside of her so that she could release that awaiting healing for her heart. I pray she knew she was enough and that she was loved so much. I pray that she could look back on that little girl that she was -- all the pain and lost feelings -- and know that she was so very special. God was keeping her here for a reason. I never knew her thoughts. I never knew how deep her pain penetrated her soul. I cannot even imagine, and I wish she were still here on this earth so that I could reach out to her, hug her, and love on her, allowing her to let it out and know that, despite all, she will never be rejected by the Father, and that He purposed her to live in this world, and great things would come out of her.

How do you handle what you deem as disrespectful? Disrespect to your culture, and specific disrespect towards your family and your spouse. How do you begin to find yourself among the rubble of distrust, hurt feelings, betrayal, and painful rejection? She was so very loved and is so very missed. "For you did not receive the spirit of bondage again to fear, but you received the Spirit of adoption by whom we cry out, "Abba, Father." The Spirit Himself bears witness with our spirit that we are children of God" (Romans 8:15-16, NKJV).

CHAPTER 3
WHO DO I BELIEVE I AM?

*"Call to Me, and I will answer you, and show you great
and mighty things, which you do not know."*
(Jeremiah 33:3, NKJV)

Where Lies Your Belief? Help My Unbelief!

Many children and families are destroyed by their beliefs
and lack of understanding of who they were created to be.
It took me a very long time to realize and understand my
identity and gain the confidence that I now have in who
God called and created me to be. It was a long lesson in
reprograming my mind to understand who I consider
myself to be, why that was, and then understand I am not
what others believe or declare to be my identity. When you
believe that you cannot accomplish something in life, more
than not, you will not. As parents, we need to speak into our
children before they even enter into this world. We need
to not only call them forth, but we need to speak out who
God said they are. We need to declare their gifts and the
promises of God over them instead of speaking curses out
of our mouths over the little blessings that we have been
given.

Often I find myself witnessing parents out with their
children, and I have witnessed children called names and
even cursed at right there in the store or wherever they
happen to be. The first thing that crosses my mind is if this
is how they are treated and spoken to out in public, there is
no telling what is said in the home.

I remember a couple of years ago, when the flu was running rampant through our community, medical professions were stressing not covering your mouth with your hands but sneezing in your elbow or tissue. One day, I was walking into a store, and a mother and her children were walking out. This little boy sneezed and did not cover his mouth. Immediately his mother yelled at him. "Boy, I will snatch your lips off if you don't cover your mouth."

Not only did she scare this little boy, but the mother also scared and stunned me speechless. The first thought that came to my mind was, did you teach him and speak to him about the correct way to sneeze, to cough, and to wash his hands, or are you assuming he should know. By her tone, both he and his siblings more than likely heard this type of language all the time. My heart went out to him as our eyes locked. I attempted to give him a compassionate nod, wanting and praying it would be ok for him. Yet, I am sure this is the life he will continue to endure until something changes.

Children need parents to not only love them, but they need to train and guide them for success. They must speak into their children and call out of their babies who they are to be. Life and death are in the power of the tongue. You are creating your world with the words that come out of your mouth. If you want success, speak success. If you want to achieve all God has already placed in you, begin to believe it, and more importantly, begin to speak it out of your mouth, regardless of what it looks like in the natural. Do you know what you see does not have to stay the same? It does not have to continue going in the direction that it is traveling. But you got to speak it. You must declare it for it to change. If you do not begin to change what is coming out of your mouth, one thing is for sure: you will continue to have what you said and continue to say. Also, the world you have created is what will continue to exist for you. Change your thinking, change you believe, change your words. "The thief does not come except to steal, and to kill, and to destroy. I have come that they may have life and that they may have it more abundantly" (John 10:10, NKJV).

Your Spoken Words

Have you ever had a conversation in your head to the point where you get upset and start thinking negatively about the situation or individual without even realizing that the thoughts you were having were unreasonable or unwarranted? Even if something had occurred where your decision – in your mind – may warrant an unpleasant thought, your decision to think negatively can, at times, be emotionally charged. Once you've concentrated and grabbed hold of the negative thought, your emotions then kick in, and the action that follows often isn't good. The enemy is a mastermind of playing on emotions, making what you think you see and believe to be twisted. See, we have been studied. He knows what will get us upset. Our areas of vulnerability have been exposed based on our previous reactions and life challenges. "Death and life are in the power of the tongue, and those who love it will eat its fruit" (Proverbs 18:21, NKJV). Guard your mouth and thoughts, and set your expectations on the things, beliefs, and words of the Lord. Speak life!

As parents, our responsibility is to speak victory over our family, our children, and their future! Parents must speak purpose and confidence to their children. Children need to understand how to handle and endure all they will go through. "These things I have spoken to you, that in Me you may have peace. In the world you will have tribulation, but be of good cheer, I have overcome the world" (John 16:33, NKJV).

We all will go through. We are supposed to say that we are going through and coming out victorious on the other side. Speaking into the lives of our children is not hard to do. It's very easy. "You are victorious! You can do all things. You are smart, beautiful, and accomplished. You will not fail; you will accomplish all God called you to do." The hard part is with the adults because before a person can speak, they must also believe it not only for their children but for themselves as well.

If a person believes that they cannot accomplish anything in life or are not capable, they will be afraid to even try. If you believe you will fail before you begin, you will never even attempt to begin. Often, we witness adults calling their children names that they believe are innocent, but nothing is innocent about them being called stupid, dumb, ignorant, or ugly, or being told that they cannot do anything right and that they will not amount to anything.

In my life, was I scared? Yes! I was scared to make a decision and stand by what or who I believed in. I was afraid to speak out or ask questions. I was afraid of rejection and did not want to reject others. Fear can stop people in their tracks. It can stop you from not only challenging yourself but it can stop you from walking in your God-given calling and dreams.

Being afraid can sabotage your dreams and desires from ever taking off. You are finished before you even began. What you say to yourself matters even more than what is said to you. However, what you say to yourself or believe about yourself stems from your environment and what was spoken over you. It comes full circle for the good and the bad. These hurtful and hateful words are now framing the world that children will live in. It has forced them to not believe they will ever be enough nor have the ability to accomplish anything. As I got older, I squashed all those dreams and just lived the life that was in front of me without continuing to ask myself who I was and what I desired to be.

I used to say to myself, "You are nothing but a dreamer. You're just dreaming all the time." Yes, this is what I said to myself, and I was embarrassed because, at a young age, I didn't understand that it was ok for me to dream. That my dreams are God-given. Not dreaming is not the answer, and not allowing our children to dream is not the answer. The answer is having a clear picture of what your dreams and desires are and the necessary and reasonable steps that must be taken to keep that dream and vision alive.

How do you help a child overcome this issue? Give them the ability to have faith and trust in who God has created them to be. How do we find who we are despite negative energy, negative attitudes, and negative comments cast our way? We tell them just how awesome they are. You affirm in their spirit not only how important they are but how much they mean to everyone. You allow them to see your heart as you speak from your heart. You permit others to live the best life they can, with no regrets. Those dreams and desires that they have, they must go after them.

Understanding, loving, and doing what God calls us to do and to be is what each of us should strive for every single day. However, you've got to be true to who He created you to be. It's time to look deeper! "Call to Me, and I will answer you, and show you great and mighty things, which you do not know" (Jeremiah 33:3, NKJV).

CHAPTER 4
THE WAKE-UP

"Be anxious for nothing, but in everything by prayer and supplication, with thanksgiving, let your requests be made known to God; and the peace of God, which surpasses all understanding, will guard your hearts and minds through Christ Jesus." (Philippians 4:6-7, NKJV)

Strength of the Cocoon

I do not want to assume that everyone understands the beautiful metamorphosis that occurs when the caterpillar hanging around suddenly turns into this beautiful butterfly. If you examine a caterpillar, it looks like a fat little worm with lines and can be colorful. The so-called legs of the caterpillar look like spikes along the body. I never liked touching worms and caterpillars. Anything slimy is probably not something many women are fond of. However, as a child, my daughter loved to pick these creatures up by the handful, if she could. She even got caught bringing them into the house. Yep, she was a no fear sort of little girl.

So, as I began to think about the metamorphosis that a caterpillar is said to go through, I started trying to understand the history and why this happens at all. Why did God not just make the caterpillar a butterfly in the first place, one that instantly flew or at least tried to fly? Why did it have to be birthed and then live on a leaf until it went through the transformation? As I read, I discovered that the beautiful mother butterfly births her baby on the exact leaf that the caterpillar will need to eat and derive nourishment.

This was interesting and contrary to what I thought about the caterpillar. I believed that the caterpillar spent a considerable amount of time as a caterpillar before it transformed. In the same way, how often are we looked on as one way, and yet, God has an entirely different person on the inside developing, being fed, and nourished until it's time for us to be revealed? Just like the caterpillar, its transformation is not when it wants or decides. It has to grow through some necessary stages or steps until it is ready for its release and not a moment before. I can believe that a caterpillar would want to be born a full-grown butterfly. Why not? One that is ready to take flight and feel the breeze on their little wings.

Instead, for their metamorphosis to occur, certain steps must happen for the caterpillar to transform into the strong and beautiful butterfly we all love to look at. As the caterpillar continues to eat, it also continues to grow. As it grows, they will then shed their skin. I had the impression, and many people may have this same impression, that the sheath is snug and the caterpillar has to struggle to burst out of tightly-woven skin to become stronger. However, this is not the case.

Once the caterpillar has shed its skin, and once the blood has begun to travel throughout the newly formed wings, it is now time for this beautiful butterfly to master flying. The newly released butterfly, which happens to also be full-grown, will flutter around, landing on aroma filled sweet flowers and trees with colorful leaves, repeating the process of nature, looking for a leaf to land on and lay her eggs.

We are a work in progress, and even when we believe that we have arrived, we are still very much a work in progress. That cocoon -- or the chrysalis -- kept the beautiful butterfly safe as the transformation was taking place, just as God keeps us safe as our minds and spiritual growth transform and grow when we seek Him and spend time in His presence. One of my favorite scriptures is in the Book of Psalms, "Delight thyself in the Lord, and He shall give you the desires of your heart" (Psalm 37:4, NKJV). Most of the time, people say, "Well, the Bible says that He will give me my desires. I do not understand why I'm not there yet." In our transformation period, some old things have to be torn away, and then new activated. Our old mind must become in line with God's Word and God's way. Those desires, dreams, and wants will line up with the godly desires that He had already placed within you.

As we invite the Holy Spirit in, and as we seek to go higher and learn more about our intimate relationship, our desire will then line up with the desire of God. Our desires should not be in contrast to God's will and call. Therefore, the desire for which He had already placed in us comes to light. I look at it this way -- it is already inside of you, receiving the nourishment needed for growth. Like the caterpillar that needs to feed on the one necessary type of leaf to grow, it is the same for us. Our metamorphosis comes as we seek to become connected to our power source, our creator, the One, the only true living God. The One that breathed life into us, the One that transformed into flesh, knowing it was the only way to reconcile man back to where we are supposed to be. He reestablished that broken connection through the shed innocent and precious blood of our Savior.

Watch as you seek Him, watch as you ask Him to show you, and watch as you delight yourself in the Lord. That burning desire within will began to become sharper and more well-defined in your spirit as it begins to line up with what God had already embedded in your spirit before you were ever born.

No Copycats Allowed

Our wonderful Creator fashioned you and me as a living, breathing masterpiece. Yet, there are times when it does not always feel as if we are a masterpiece at all. There was a long period of my life where it seemed like I never looked back. I did not look forward, and yet I did not look back. I stayed in a circle, going around and around.

There is an old song by an old school group, the Temptations, called "Ball of Confusion." I can hear it in my head right now! The song had lyrics dealing with the fact that no one knows where the world is headed and how the perpetual wheel of a confused life just continued to spin and spin, with no end in sight. Some of the lyrics are what we are witnessing today:
"they speak about demonstrations, humiliations, segregations, suicide from bills, revolution, gun control and cities on fire, and unemployment rising, everything in a state
of confusion, and no one cares. It is funny how that song speaks about the life this world is in right now. It speaks the truth about so many issues taking place in this day and age right now."

As I grew up, I remember my life was this hamster wheel, and when you are not seeking God, and I was not, this is what it turns into. I was not asking the questions; I did not understand who I was, nor what I should be looking for in life. I was not getting any worthwhile answers. After all, if you do not know what to ask, you will get the answer to what you asked, right, wrong, or indifferent. Life felt indifferent. Life felt meaningless and idle. Not going up, not going down, just a state of a confused mind, one that did not know or understand who she was. When a person does not know or understand who they are, the world will try to tell you who you are or who you should be, and what you should be doing with your life. It is not hard to be a copycat. Being a copycat is much easier than living the life you have been chosen and called for. It is easier to be a copycat than to walk out your path, the chosen path that God has for you. It is easier to settle for where you are instead of choosing to go after what God called you to be. But you have to know for yourself who that is. It is imperative to seek God in this area. If not, you will never have that understanding of the road that you should be traveling, which may not be the easy path.

The God-chosen path is not always easy, and often, it is not always desired by most. There are a lot of people who reject or run away from what they have been called to do. Nonetheless, if this is what you have been called to do, you will continue searching for the peace and happiness that you know is missing from your life until your desires line up with the Lord's. The world cannot fulfill this desire. A job you choose may not fulfill this desire. Even your education that provides you with a lucrative living may not fulfill you. Only what you do for God will quench that which is lying dormant inside of your spirit.

Me – I'll Take Sushi

I have a beautiful, blessed, smart, and creative daughter. I knew that she was talented at a young age, and as she has grown and matured, those talents and abilities within her have prospered. As a little girl, she had been very strong-willed. I remember having to pray over her because of how strong-willed she was. I would never desire her to be like I was growing up. I learned to appreciate her strength and all she has accomplished and still desires to accomplish.

After we moved from New Jersey to Georgia, my daughter found herself in a new school environment. She had only attended schools affiliated with the military. I must say this, and I hope it is understood correctly, the geographic makeup of our current school system here in Georgia (Atlanta metropolitan area) does not compare to the Department of Defense schools.

In the first couple of days of high school, my daughter's teacher gave the class an assignment to write certain facts about themselves. What she did not say was that they were going to share this information with their classmates. My daughter loved skateboarding and Shaun White, who at that time was a famous pro-skateboarder. Since she grew up in Okinawa Japan, she also loved sushi, amongst other things.

My daughter explained that she was being honest concerning what she wrote down. She thought it would be personal, and maybe the teacher would read it, but that was it. So, she was very surprised when her teacher started calling on the kids in her class to stand up and read what they had written down.

When the teacher called her name to share what she had written, the class made fun of her and started making "eew" sounds concerning her choices. My strong and independent daughter did not miss a beat. She turned around and said, "I'm sorry it is not chicken." Well, I guess that ended that. When she told me what happened, even knowing how she was, I was a little surprised. I said to her jokingly, "Are you trying to make friends at all here at this school?"

This incident taught me volumes. It showed me how this young black girl was not afraid to stand up for what she believed, regardless of what others thought. Who cared what they thought, and who cared what they said? What is most important is what you say to yourself -- in your head and aloud about yourself. That is what matters. Not the opinions of others that do not know you, your experiences, or your heart.

I had to learn that everyone does not get to walk with you. Everyone does not get to take up your time, and everyone is not for you. How many times have you accomplished something in your life, and you really thought, I'm doing so good? This was a lot of hard work, yet those around you, even family members, do not recognize your worth? Jesus was not accepted in His own home. "Then He said, 'Assuredly, I say to you, no prophet is accepted in his own country'" (Luke 4:24, NKJV). He was not accepted because of the familiarity. Unfortunately, familiarity keeps others from appreciating you and congratulating you on your accomplishments.

What the Lord spoke in my spirit was, "She will need to be strong for the times in which she is living." When I looked at my daughter, she possessed so much confidence in herself as a child. As a teenager growing up on military bases and moving around the world, she was still able to walk and interact in this confidence. Sure, she knew she had parents who loved her, cherished her, and would do right by her and her brother. I'm very certain that having a loving family behind you, supporting you in what you desire to do, makes a world of difference. I understand this because I did not have this in my life.

I made a mental note, and I paid attention to the difference between the life my daughter lived and the life I lived as I grew up. I remember thinking about how very different our childhoods were. I'm also quite sure all parents can say to themselves, "I wish I did better. I wish I knew more. I wish I would have instilled even more wisdom and understanding into my children than what I did." It took me a very long time to find my voice, and it took me even longer to understand my identity and what God created me to do in this life.

CHAPTER 5
CREATED FOR GREATNESS

"Therefore, if anyone is in Christ, the new creation has come: The old has gone, the new is here." (2 Corinthians 5:17, NIV)

Made in His Image- Not Just Dust

Children love to play dress up. "I want to be the doctor. No, I want to be the fireman. I want to be the mother or daddy," declares the voices of our innocent children. The innocence of a child is priceless. Children have the ability to easily identify with what they like or are with no fear. They have the belief that it is theirs for the taking, and no one will stop them from making it happen. How awesome it is to have this innocent belief, without the knowledge of fear and doubt?

It is very strange because the more I look back, I do not remember wanting to play pretend as a child. How exactly do children know who they are to be? Were they supposed to tell me? We all go through cycles in our lives. Trials and tribulations come our way, and some of us can muster through, while others faint along the wayside, never to rise again. How do some of us make it and others give up? What is inside of our being, which gives us the fortitude to keep going, to keep fighting, to keep standing, to keep walking, to keep running the race, and never losing heart?

Finding who we are is not a fact that everyone discovers. Was I created to be or do anything? My mind had asked that question far too often. Thank goodness my heart did not act on the thoughts of my mind.

Attempting to figure out who I am and then develop the belief system to go along with the knowledge is not always as easy as it may appear to be. Unfortunately, some people may never discover who they are, while others come to know it and disregard it. As a believer of the Word of God, He has laid out who we were created to be and our purpose. We are to be that vessel that leads others to the Father, not a stumbling block for those that are struggling in their belief.

I remember hearing a pastor teaching one day on this principle of walking in your calling as opposed to copying off someone else only because it sounded like a good career or a venture. We all have to know, seek, and understand what is for each of us. For example, Sheila has been blessed in a certain area with a special talent. She simply loves what she does. She is motivated, passionate, and great at what she does. She is walking, working, and anointed in her God-given calling.

Sheila is where she is supposed to be. Her good friend, Emily, likes what Sheila does. Emily always hears the excitement in Sheila's voice. Although Sheila also tells Emily about her battles, Emily thinks that Sheila is always on the winning side. She sees the reward that Sheila receives and decides she wants to do the same thing.

Emily believes she can do it too and receive the same blessings as Sheila, even though she was not called to do the same. It is possible that Emily could do it or even be more successful, but that is not where her anointing is. God purposed something in Sheila's heart that was only for her to do and gave her the grace to accomplish it.

We are to do the work He called and created us to do. Can it be that people see and recognize the talents and success of someone else and want to do that thing, even if it is not their calling? Yes, they can. However, that does not make it right. He called Emily to be a teacher, to encourage and speak life into young lives. Emily rejected the notion of teaching for more money and a more glamorous life. Sheila loved her adventurous life, while Emily, who sought to do the exact same thing, found herself unfulfilled and unhappy.

God declared His goodness on His creation. Patterned after God, we are speaking spirits. The Bible declares, "Then God said, 'Let Us make man in Our image, according to Our likeness; let them have dominion over the fish of the sea, over the birds of the air, and the cattle, over all the earth and over every creeping thing that creeps on the earth.' So, God created man in His image; in the image of God He created him; male and female He created them" (Genesis 1:26-27, NKJV).

There is nothing negative about how you look, and there is nothing unpleasant about the way I look. He made each of us different. Even twins are not totally identical. Sometimes no one, except for their parents, can tell them apart. However, this denotes that there is a difference. God knows us the same way. He created, called, and equipped us. He knows who we are and loves us the same.

I have a T-shirt that says, "Jesus loves you, but I'm His favorite." I wear that T-shirt every week, running around taking care of errands, and there has not been one time that I have worn it where someone has not said, "No, I'm His favorite too!" It always sounds as if they are pleading with me to understand. I simply laugh and say, "Yes, you can be that, too. You just have to believe. I do believe it, so I can say it." This statement always gets them to agree with me. Boy, if it could only be that simple to tell and teach someone just how much God loves them and who they are in Christ Jesus. Can you imagine how it would be? The Bible says, "Then Jesus called a little child to Him, set him in the midst of them, and said, 'Assuredly, I say to you, unless you are converted and become as little children, you will by no means enter the kingdom of heaven. Therefore, whoever humbles himself as this little child is the greatest in the kingdom of heaven'" (Matthew 18:2-4, NKJV).

Each of us, regardless of our race, is made special in His sight. Our color is beautiful to God. Brown eyes, blue eyes, green eyes, we are all beautiful in His eyes. His eyes are the ones that matter. Yet, men in their wisdom, believe it is permissible to mistreat another person merely because of their race or origin. It is not acceptable! He calls us to love our neighbor just like we do ourselves. "So, he answered and said, 'You shall love the Lord your God with all your heart, with all your soul, with all your strength, and with all your mind, and your neighbor as yourself'" (Luke 10:27, NKJV).

I searched the Bible via the internet and found that there were 46 verses where he commanded us to love others. God commanded us to love one another. His desire is for us to treat each other with love, respect, and honor. What we should not do is strive to purposely cause hurt, harm, and danger to others. Yet, most people do not even understand just how wonderful and beautiful we each are. Everyone one of us is special in His sight, and we have been created for greatness. We have been created for a purpose. It is up to us to believe this for ourselves. Special, and a peculiar, people whom Father God loves so much. So much so that He sent His only Son to bring us back to Him. The Bible tells us in Proverbs that hatred is the culprit that stirs up strife, but love is able to cover that sin if we just love ourselves and others just as God loves us.

Begin to love yourself! Start by looking in your mirror. Study yourself, study your beautiful face. Look at where your eyes are. Look at the shape of your nose, the twist of your mouth. Count all the freckles. You know, the ones that you probably used to hate. Now, close your eyes and think about how God sees you. Think about how He knows all the little freckles on your nose; he put them there, and He loves each and every little one of them. Think about how God loves even the things you may not like about yourself. It is what makes you, you. You are loved! You are a special creation of the Father. "Before I formed you in the womb, I knew you; Before you were born, I sanctified you; I ordained you a prophet to the nations" (Jeremiah 1:5, NKJV).

Your Greatness is Showing

It is time for us all to take a deep, long look at our lives and the path that we are now traveling. Why have we ended up where we are now? Often, when I considered my life, and in the process, I started to wonder why I think the way I think, why I get so upset at certain things that are beyond my control. As I said before, I do not remember my thoughts as a child of what I desired to be or do in life. I do not even recall saying that I wanted to be married or that I wanted to be a doctor or nurse. Even when I did go to college right after high school, I did not have a clue as to what I desired to do. I just knew that college was supposed to be the next step, a means to an end.

My decision to study nursing was not a decision at all. I just figured that since my mother worked at a hospital, I may as well do the same thing. After all, I would love to be able to help people that are hurting and in need. I'm sure some people can relate to the same experience. You believe you are doing the right thing because others are doing it, and that is a great expectation to have, but is it right for you?

I forged ahead and attempted my college education. One day, and I cannot remember where I was, but I do remember thinking, what makes you think you can be a nurse; you will not know what to do, and you will probably kill someone. This thought scared me, but it made sense. I immediately agreed with the thought. I should not be doing this. What do I know? I will probably do something wrong and hurt someone. At that moment, I had decided I no longer wanted to be a nurse, but what now and what next? This is how cunning and slick the enemy can be. This is how our thought life can be railroaded to make decisions that will take us in a completely different direction.

Another way that situations and faulty thinking can come against us, attempting to rob us of what we have been called to do in this life, is by discouragement. My desire in life, I thought, was to be the best wife, the best mother, the best Christian, but something was missing. The Word says He knew us before we were even born. "Before I formed you in the womb, I knew you; Before you were born, I sanctified you; I ordained you a prophet to the nations" (Jeremiah 1:5, NKJV). It had taken me a very long time to realize that not only was I not living the life that God created me to live. Nor was I even positioned in the place He had for me to be in, nor doing all that I should be doing, fulfill what God has laid out for me. I was still very unhappy with my life, I knew I was still not fulfilled, and now I had become discouraged concerning the course my life was taking.

Can you say the same thing? Have you ever stopped and sought God concerning your life, who you are, and where He has destined for you to be? Are you doing what you were created to do, or are you merely existing and just moving through life with no passion for living the life He has called and created you to live? You know your life does not have to remain in the pit one more day. You do not have to continue to settle for the booth in the back when he has called you to dine at the captain's table. Upgrade your thinking, upgrade your expectations, and upgrade your exuberance for the things that God has in store for you to accomplish.

While we were stationed overseas in Okinawa, I had started taking college classes again. I had no particular direction, and I chose business classes, not knowing why. I believed that once I took enough classes, I could figure it all out. Since I was starting over, I had to take a psychology class. I used to like these sorts of classes in high school, so surely, I would like them in college. Well, let me just say, my professor for this class was not very exciting. He stood in the class with his back to the students and wrote on every blackboard filling it up and lectured at almost a whisper.

Once finished, he would go back to the first board and start writing all over again. This was the entire class. I did not do very well on my midterm exam. I knew I had to do better to pass the class.

Before I could finish the class, I received a Red Cross notification that my father was not expected to live. He had just been diagnosed with pancreatic cancer. After two weeks of him being in the hospital, he was released to go home and was told there was nothing else that could be done. Finding this out, I had to leave Japan and get back to Pennsylvania as fast as I could. I contacted the school, and even having a Red Cross notification, they still told me there was nothing they could do because this professor was retiring at the end of the class and leaving the island after the final exam was administered -- only he could administer the exam. Therefore, I would have to resign from the class.

I was madder than I was upset about having to withdraw from the class. I was already not doing that great in the class due to a horrible instructor, and now I was being told I have to withdraw when all I wanted to do was finish. On top of that, my father was dying, and I needed to do everything possible to get there to see him, to pray with him, and to let him know how much I loved him. I was discouraged, sad, and hurting inside. This school couldn't care less that my father is terminally ill. My experience has been so bad. I would never retake that class. I would CLEP the class. I would do what I had to do, but I would not sit in that class again after my experience.

When my daughter decided to go to a Christian University, I started looking at the curriculum and what they had to offer.

Again, I thought, well, I still want to go to school. I guess I will just pick up with the business classes that I left off with. Even attending a Christian college did not solve my issue of being lost because I was not asking God for answers. Years later, when I finally started seeking, praying, and asking, I received the answer. I got my lightbulb moment. At least, that is what it felt like for me.

My desire had always been helping, encouraging, praying with and for others, and trying to help them resolve an issue in their lives. What I discovered was counseling. Then I discovered that the same school had Christian Counseling. Well, I did not know there was such a thing, let alone Crisis Counseling. After I had checked into it and applied, I was told I would have to take psychology and get a degree in it. Do not ask me why, but I simply did not realize "Christian" counseling was a part of psychology.

I had said to myself, that I was never sitting in a psychology class again, and when I said it, I meant it. I had the memories of being in that awful class and not there when my dad passed away. My mind linked them together as a horrible event that truly hurt my heart. This is what I mean about our thoughts. What we tell ourselves and believe about ourselves has to come from somewhere. Often our minds can be trapped and trampled on by the negative world we live in and those around us.

When we allow the enemy to take up residence in our minds, and when we do not have an understanding of who we are and what we are called to do, we can go through life and miss the mark altogether. My almost missed opportunity was when I told myself that I would never again take a

Psychology class ever again. This decision was based on a very sad and hurtful experience that occurred at the very time I was in a Psychology class overseas when my father became ill and was hospitalized. Within a very short period of time, he was diagnosed with Pancreatic cancer and passed away two short weeks later.

The passing of my father has always been entangled with me having that horrible experience in school and blaming it on that awful psychology professor (his class was pretty bad). I was declaring without even realizing it that I was saying no to something that God had already put His yes on and called me to do. God had prepared for me to complete this course for my life purpose. I praise and thank Him for blessing me to do just that. Way back when I had graduated from high school and enrolled in college for nursing, my minor was in psychology. Perhaps instead of just dropping the nursing course, maybe I would have found my way to the Psychology department way back when, but that simply is not how my story played out. I had to go up the hill and get pushed back, tumbling upside down, just to find myself on the right side of the "right" hill.

It was not until I started seeking that He said, "Ok, she's ready now. She's ready to hear, she's ready to listen, and she's willing to obey." Are you ready to seek the Father, allowing the Holy Spirit to operate and just take over, as you follow His lead? It is time to get ready. The state of the world needs us. People need what we have, and people need what we can help them understand in their life. We cannot waste another minute of the time we have left, for no man knows the day or the time that God will return. We need to be ready! It is time, my dear friend. It is your time, too!

Experiences happen to us in life, like the passing away of someone we love -- a parent, a spouse, and even a child. The pain can cut so deep that you feel the pressure in your chest. Your heart feels like it is going to explode as you wonder why. There is nothing that escapes our Father, our awesome Father, who loves us so very much. Still, we are on this earth, living out the life that we have been purposed to live, and our life on earth will not be eternal. One day as the last breath escapes our body, our spirit will transition to one of two places.

CHAPTER 6
SHUTTING THE DOOR ON THE PAST

*"For He shall give His angels charge over you, to keep you
in all your ways. In their hands, they shall bear you up,
lest you dash
your foot against a stone." (Psalm 91: 11-12, NKJV)*

Courage to Live

Have you ever felt like giving up in life? Throwing in the
towel, not even trying one more time? Have you had the
rug pulled out from under you, leaving you breathless and
in unbelief, concerning whatever the situation was that
occurred? Have you ever believed that you have done all
you can do in whatever the life situation is, and this is it? A
person with a negative mind, and defeatist set of beliefs, can
not only bring another down, but they can talk someone out
of the dream inside of you. Their belief that nothing ever
works, or that it works for others, not just themselves or
even for you, can ultimately make you quit. It can make you
give up and give in.

Stop thinking now, right now! Begin to speak the Word of
God in your life, over your thoughts, and over the situation
that is happening to in and to your family. He has good for us,
but we must believe that it is for us and can indeed happen
in our situation. It can make you question your desires and
life choices. You can talk yourself out of anything, even the
good things and purposes of life. At the same time, you can
also be talked out of your dreams and the visions you have
for your life, especially if you do not guard your heart and
guard your mind.

It is never easy when you find yourself around those who are speaking death into every situation, regardless of how big or how small, while you continue to speak and believe life. It is also not easy to attempt to try to shelter your heart, to protect your mind, and guard your ears from hearing those things that are contrary to what God says about you. It is not always easy to stay in "the land of positive," believing that just as others have achieved success in life, you can also achieve your dreams. When the circumstances around you make you feel defeated, or perhaps your mind tells you that you are a loser and not capable of achieving any good thing, instead of validating what you are feeling and allowing your mind to believe those lies, this is when you must begin to speak to yourself, even out loud. You must learn to change your environment. Change your circle of influence for the better...for your better. But what if the negative is in your own family? What if the negativity is coming from those who should be holding you up and cheering you on? It happens, my friend, and we all have to find the right solution for our circumstances so that we can maintain our peace and keep our dreams alive in our hearts.

Our only hope is in the Lord and the Word of God. When it comes down to it, our success, as well as our failure, lies in our belief. I have found that it is much easier to give up than to keep pushing. With giving up, you get that false sense of peace because after giving up, what is next? The struggle that was taking place in your life, tying up your emotions, and causing you to exert the pressure of daily pushing on to your purpose, ends when you give up. Unfortunately, you are now left in the wondering state of uncertainty, stretching into uncompleted accomplishments, unsatisfied results, and broken commitments. The false sense of peace will not last too long before your next challenge presents itself in a different form. Will the next outcome be the same? Will every outcome be the same, or will you and will I gather the courage inside of us to step into the faith that we have inside? It can be small faith, but even small faith can turn into great faith.

"So, Jesus said to them, 'Because of your unbelief; for assuredly, I say to you, if you have faith as a mustard seed, you will say to this mountain, 'Move from here to there,' and it will move; and nothing will be impossible for you'" (Matthew 17:20, NKJV).

Being emotionally led is yet another area that drives our decision making and behavior. I can honestly say that I believe a lot of people are emotionally driven. What we think, say, do, and believe often stems from life experiences and our emotions. It's not that all emotions are bad, but you can't allow your emotions to rule your life. Being emotionally led can potentially lead a person down a very destructive road. When emotions are not checked, bad and unfavorable decisions can and will be made. The definition of the word emotions from the dictionary states: "Emotions means a mental state that arises spontaneously rather than through conscious effort and is often accompanied by physiological changes; a feeling: the emotions of joy, sorrow, reverence, hate, and love. A state of mental agitation or disturbance. The part of the consciousness that involves feeling, sensibility. The mental state of agitation and disturbance." Within this definition, we can see why the Word of God tells us to keep our minds stayed on Christ to have that desired peace. "You will keep him in perfect peace, whose mind is stayed on You because he trusts in You" (Isaiah

26:3, NKJV). Regardless, a person's emotions can often stem from a specific incident that occurred, or perhaps an argument or confrontation that took place. Rejection or a breakup can also play a part in this emotional struggle. The bottom line is that making decisions without truly thinking it through can lead to serious issues for everyone involved.

As believers, we must seek the wisdom and peace of God in all things. However, oftentimes, this is not done, especially when emotions have been allowed to make the decision for us. There is not a day that goes by where a tragic situation is not reported on the news. Gun violence directed in places of employment by a disgruntled employee that was fired, or divorces, domestic abuse, child abuse, and even road rage has just about taken over our nation's roads due to drivers becoming angry when other drivers allegedly upset them. To the majority of people, this does not even make sense. Unfortunately, it happens every day across the nation.

Emotionally led decision making can also lead to issues such as overspending and even mistreating other people. Often, we hear about serious and even deadly incidents that occurred when one person became so angry that they attempted or even succeeded in harming or ending the life of another person. If only they had taken a breath and stepped away to pray and seek God concerning what should or should not be done, they would have made the best decision.

Hence, we go about our daily lives, attempting to justify our emotional decisions or mistakes, while many lives have been ruined because of another person's emotions from a bad situation that took place, causing them to make decisions that they would not have made had it been under a different circumstance. It is easy to look back at what should have been done concerning all decisions. The Word tells us to let this mind be in you that is also in Christ Jesus. When we are Christ-focused and Holy Spirit led, our emotions can be controlled. This is exactly what should occur. We are to yield to the Holy Spirit for the direction and comfort that we need. I've had to learn to identify my emotions and take a step back from situations happening in my life. Removing yourself from the situation by taking a walk, praying, or calling a friend can help. Anything that can be done should be done if it can take a person's mind off the situation at hand and allow it to be in a different, more positive light. "But seek first the kingdom of God and His righteousness, and all these things shall be added to you" (Matthew 6:33, NKJV).

Believing His Love - You Are Worthy

Have you ever heard the saying, "your health is your wealth?" I had a very serious health scare that happened back in 2004. The decision by my husband to retire from the Air Force was a relief; it also became an extremely stressful situation for my family. Our family was about to venture into a place we had never been to before. My husband and I got married really young, right after he went into the Air Force. So, he had never had a job or career outside of the Air Force. I tried to quietly and mentally deal with all the uncertainty. Were we going to be ok? Were we going to have enough money still coming into our home? It all became too stressful. I quietly held everything inside, even my thoughts. On the inside, I was an emotional mess, and yet no one ever knew it. I did not share my fears with anyone, and that included my husband. I believed that he had enough on his mind, without me adding the extra fear that I was dealing with to his plate as well. So, I did what I thought a wife should do, I prayed and kept it to myself.

Finally, when my husband did receive a position, and he received it very quickly, it seemed like an answer to our prayers. Talk about thankful. The only problem was he hated it. As I think back, it was awful for him. He hated the unstructured nature of the organization he was attached to. He also did not care for the supervisor in charge, because after all, as a military veteran, he knew what good management and supervision was, and that was not taking place in that organization. My husband would come home every day after work, he would be there when I got home, and I remember it as if it were yesterday. I would be standing in the kitchen, starting dinner, as he filled me in on the craziness of his day. I literally just stood there and listened to him go on and on and on. This went on for the first two weeks he worked there, and by the third week, that is when it happened. I became extremely ill; all the stress and an infection had taken a toll on my body.

I thought I had the flu, but unbeknownst to me, I had an extremely elevated blood sugar level brought on by an infection that I had developed. This illness caught me and my family off guard. I was unaware of this issue taking place in my body, as well as my doctor. I had just had an appointment with my doctor two weeks prior. Every symptom I had should have been a signal that something was wrong, but it was missed by me, my husband, and my doctor.

I started to have issues with my vision. I thought it was because of my glasses. People had even told me that I was losing weight, but I always responded by saying, "Well, I should be. I'm doing my best to lose weight. I'm walking and drinking a ton of water." My husband and I were members of a wonderful church in New Jersey, and we were attending their Bible Institute classes every Saturday morning. I had heard about how oxygenated water was good for your body and helped with weight loss. So, you know what I did? I found a store not far from our church that sold it.

After the class, we would stop past this natural herb store, and I would buy a case of oxygenated water, and my weight loss journey began. So, yeah, my clothes were falling off me. I was tired, and I looked like I was wasting away. But remember, I thought that was a good thing. That just meant this "special water" was working. I was one happy sister! "But whoever drinks of the water that I shall give him will never thirst. But the water that I shall give him will become in him a fountain of water springing up into everlasting life." (John 4:14, NKJV).

After about a week of not feeling well, for which I thought I had the flu, my blood sugar levels shot up to dangerously high levels! I was still walking, talking, driving, cooking, working, praying, and doing everything else I needed to do, tired and all. When that illness attempted to shut down my body, my boldness in Christ was birthed out in full force. Without going into too much detail concerning my health scare, I ended up in ICU.

My husband had driven me to my doctor's office, since like I said, we thought I had the flu. Once there, panic erupted when the medical assistant was not able to set me up for an EKG. I was still awake, but I kept wanting to sleep as my alertness began to fade. The next thing I know, they were calling the ambulance to take me to the hospital. Once in the ambulance, I was told that my blood sugar had to be over 500 because they were not able to get a proper read on it, but they would do so once we got to the emergency room.

Now, once in the emergency room, they tested my blood sugar. This is where all the shock came in. The tech said, as if I had a clue of what he was talking about, "Your blood sugar is 1,861." Silence. Staring. Finally, I spoke.

"Reallllly?"

He looked up at me crazily and asked, "Did you know you can go into a coma at 500?"

"No, I did not know, and why do you think I should know this?"

At this point, I was so confused. See, I had not started taking any medication, even for being what they considered "borderline." I believe the mix-up and lack of informed knowledge occurred because it happened right when my husband retired. I had medical records at the base clinic, and I now had a great physician off base who was running tests.

I had been told I was borderline for whatever that meant to me at the time, but that was it. That is why I was drinking water, trying to eat healthily, cut out sugar, and walking. I was excited because I believed everything I was doing was working so I could move away from the borderline to healed. To make it even more miraculous, I had a nurse that told me she was called in to be my special nurse and take care of me. These were her exact words, and this is exactly what she did.

Of course, I was given an IV, and by midnight that night, when she came into the room to test my blood sugar level, it was well below 150. I remember seeing my angel, my nurse, in front of the window on the other side of the room, holding the tester up in the air and dancing around in a half-circle with the tester raised in the air. I lifted my left arm and said, "Praise Jesus," and went back to sleep. That was my last time seeing my beautiful angel in the flesh. "Do not forget to entertain strangers, for by so doing some have unwittingly entertained angels" (Hebrews 13:2, NKJV).

As I was in the hospital recovering, it did not take long for me to come to understand my purpose and my calling, what it is that I'm on this earth to do. If you had come within arm's reach of me, and they did because everyone wanted to see the woman with the 1800 blood sugar level, I would tell you that God loves me, and I am a child of the Most-High God. I knew without a doubt that God loved me, saved me, and kept me here for His purpose. I knew then and right there that life is too precious and too short to waste time not being and doing what God called and created us to be. That is when the real praying and the real asking began, making it personal, asking God to show me, to please show me and lead me.

Now, even with all this taking place in my life, I was very embarrassed. I was embarrassed because of how sick I had gotten. I was so worried about what people thought.

Did they believe I was reckless or that I did not care about myself or my family?

As the weeks and months went on, there was not a day that went by that I did not think about my purpose or try to understand what I had been created for. I wanted to talk about God's grace, healing, mercy, and His angel that He sent to take care of me. I wanted to tell others of how the night before I became so ill, I was in the church at our Encounter with God retreat for three days. I wanted to share how when I came home that night, I was lying in bed, and as I tried to sleep, it was as if my body was lifted. I was stretched out with a glowing cloth all around me as I was praising the Father.

I had found my voice. I knew in my being when my body was laid back in my bed, and I continued to sleep, that He healed and cleansed me. He knew what was taking place. He knew because He is our Jehovah Rapha – the Lord that heals. He is El Elyon – the Most-High God. He is Jehovah Shammah, the Lord who is ever-present with us. My fire, the fire inside of me, was still burning. He was refining me; He had given me the courage to walk with no condemnation. He is my everything.! "Surely, He has borne our griefs and carried our sorrows; Yet we esteemed Him stricken, smitten by God, and afflicted. But He was wounded for our transgressions, He was bruised for our iniquities; The chastisement for our peace was upon Him, and by His stripes, we are healed" (Isaiah 53:4-5, NKJV). We must never allow our lives to become so stressed, so overworked, so worried and so afraid, that sickness begins to creep in, stealing of our health and our peace of mine. I regret to this day, that I allowed it to happen, that I did not stop and breath, that I did not notice me. I did not pay enough attention to my mind, my body and to my heart. My own self-care was neglected, as I sought out to be there for everyone else. As we live and as we learn, we should also strive to survive the lesson.

We must be focused on our Father and the things of God at all times and above all things. We cannot do the work when we are ill, and stressed out over the issues of life.

One Sunday afternoon, after our church service, once I had recovered, I was at a women's bible study. I wanted to share my miracle of healing with everyone, but I was shut down by another sister in Christ who was in charge. She immediately made a statement as if to say, "This is why we need to take care of ourselves and not be so unhealthy," or something to this effect. What my ears heard was, "Shame on you, Denise. How dare you not take care of the temple God gave you."

At that point, I felt nothing but shame and embarrassment. All the love and joy I had in my heart felt as if it had been squeezed out. She proceeded to lecture me, and all in attendance, about the importance of our health as if I did not already know. I mean, come on. I spent a week in the hospital in ICU because of my lack of knowledge and attention concerning my health and the stress I was attempting to suppress. I get it! But I wanted to share about our wonderful and loving Jesus.

I needed so badly to share Jesus! I wanted to share how I felt in basking in the knowledge of His love and how I realized at that moment just how much He loved me! But I stopped sharing. I shut up, and I shut down. I made a decision that I would no longer speak about what happened. After that, if I did share, it was only if I believed I was led to do so. Other than that, I told myself that I would keep my mouth shut about what happened in my life.

This was a very unfortunate decision on my part. The hurt I felt from another sister in Christ lingered and brought up those old wounds and doubts. I was embarrassed, because now in my eyes, it looked as if I must not care about my family since I allowed myself to become ill. Those were the thoughts that ran through my head, keeping me from speaking, writing, and being the person that God had called me to be. I did not believe that I was good enough, regardless of my miraculous experience. Her tongue of judgment pierced my heart. The judgmental and condescending attitude I experienced left a faulty impression in my heart, one that would take some time to get past. In addition, it would also take a considerable amount of time for me to forgive myself so that I could learn to move on fearlessly. The self-doubt and the guilt for me were so very real.

There are times in life where it may not be easy to maintain our faith because of life situations. Every day will not be a bed of roses. Everyone will go through the ups and downs of life, and there will also be occurrences when things can become extremely difficult. I used to be so afraid of fear that I would not speak of it. I often heard others tell those dealing with issues that they just needed to have faith as if that was the problem. I believe this is so very wrong to say to anyone, especially when a person has not walked in their shoes. What we as believers must do is love, pray, and have compassion for those suffering and in need.

Sowing the love of God, lending a hand, or being a friend can make a world of difference to someone that is living through something hard and hurtful. Allow God to use you where you are, to be that light for someone whose light has left their eyes. Be that smile for someone that has lost theirs and be that hope for someone who believes their life is hopeless. We never know how we may be used. Let's be open and a willing vessel ready to be used by God when needed, instead of exhibiting a critical, judgmental nature. "Finally, all of you be of one mind, having compassion for one another; love as brothers, be tenderhearted, be courteous; not returning evil for evil or reviling for reviling, but on the contrary blessing, knowing that you were called to this, that you may inherit a blessing" (1 Peter 3:8-9, NKJV).

So, what would you do, and who would you believe, when it comes to your health? How about when it comes to your spiritual calling and identity? How do you believe in something that is completely contrary to what can be seen in the natural? How would you deal with the disbelief of others towards you? What do you do when others think that your belief is unrealistic, or perhaps they even tell you that you're in denial or not living in reality? How do we handle our disappointment in those around us concerning how we are treated and how we are viewed in the eyes of man?

My sisters, we are loved children of the Most-High God! It will never be easy, but it is more than worth it when our focus and direction is only on God. Allow yourself to be directed by the Holy Spirit. Do not attempt to please man. Instead, be all you are called and created to be for Jesus! The One who has saved us, called, and equipped us, and has created us in His likeness. "'For My thoughts are not your thoughts, nor are your ways My ways,' says the Lord. 'For as the heavens are higher than the earth, so are My ways higher than your ways, and My thoughts than your thoughts'" (Isaiah 55:7-9, NKJV).

CHAPTER 7
TAKING BACK ME

"Be anxious for nothing, but in everything by prayer and supplication, with thanksgiving, let your requests be made known to God; and the peace of God, which surpasses all understanding, will guard your hearts and minds through Christ Jesus." (Philippians 4:6-7, NKJV)

Listening with Your Heart – No More Fear

"And those whose faith has made them good in God's sight must live by faith, trusting him in everything. Otherwise, if they shrink back, God will have no pleasure in them" (Hebrews 10:38-39, TLB). In the Word of God, many passages deal with fear. Fear is the opposite of faith. You can't have faith and be in fear at the same time. You can't be fearful and believe that you have faith in the Word of God.

Faith will cast away all fear. Fear is from the enemy. For believers, the word fear stands for "false expressions appearing real," the realm Satan wants you to think is real in your mind. The fear implanted in your heart to keep you from standing up and being who and all God has destined you to be. What are you afraid of? What am I afraid of?

The Word says, "we are more than conquers in Christ Jesus," and yet fear paralyzes so many of us. It can stop a person from taking that leap of faith and walking in the greatness that God has called them to. The Bible declares, "Only fear the Lord, and serve Him in truth with all your heart; for consider what great things He has done for you" (1 Samuel 12:24, NKJV). This fear means to reverence God; this is different. When we reverence God, we are loving God; we are honoring and respecting the Father.

The dictionary speaks of fear as "a feeling of agitation and anxiety caused by the presence or imminence of danger, or an unpleasant often strong emotion caused by anticipation or awareness of danger. To feel fear inside, to know what it feels like to be afraid or frightened." The time has come to not be afraid of who God created you to be.

Fear can create a state of anxiety within us. Even now, I have caught myself on edge, believing that if I prepare my mind and heart to receive what is not positive, then I will not be let down. God's Word declares, "But without faith, it is impossible to please Him, for he who comes to God must believe that He is and that He is a rewarder of those who diligently seek Him" (Hebrews 11:6, NKJV). I can then be prepared to accept the issue and the hand that I have been dealt with. I never really looked at it that way. There had been so much that occurred in my past, even as an adult, that I became more familiar with waiting for the other shoe to drop instead of automatically leaning on faith and setting my expectations on the grace and goodness of God.

I would never have believed that I was in a state of fear; however, I have felt anxious. I would never speak a word of fear or disbelief, but I had to examine my heart and see that without it being said, I had become very anxious concerning life situations that would creep up in my life.

My mind wandered back to how I have viewed different aspects of my life. I've always been anxious about something. A person can be anxious and not even realize it. We can call it being overly concerned, worked up, eager, or even restless. Regardless of what it is called, it is all anxiousness, and it all stems from fear. I was anxious to get married. I was anxious to move overseas to another country. I was anxious about raising my children. The Bible declares, "Be anxious for nothing, but in everything by prayer and supplication, with thanksgiving, let your requests be made known to God; and the peace of God, which surpasses all understanding, will guard your hearts and minds through Christ Jesus" (Philippians 4:6-7, NKJV).

Living in fear is not living a victorious life. It is past time to stand strong and not be afraid. My life and your life will not change until the mind has been renewed, changed, and/or rewired, not allowing fear and anxiousness to keep you from being overburdened and disheartened. Please believe that the enemy wants nothing more than for you and me to dismiss the dream and vision that our Father has planted in us. We should allow our light to shine so that others will see the Father in us. "He did not waver at the promise of God through unbelief but was strengthened in faith, giving glory to God, and being fully convinced that what He had promised He was also able to perform. And therefore, it was accounted to him for righteousness" (Romans 4:20-22 NKJV).

Here is a thought. Have you ever been in the company of people who always complain about something? Nothing is ever going right. Nothing will go right. The glass is always half-empty instead of half full. As soon as they open their mouths, you can already anticipate that what is going to come out of it won't be positive.

Listen, what is for you, is for you, and if you don't receive what you desire, it was not meant for you in the first place. I look at life and the issues of life in this light. If it does not happen for me, amen, and if it does happen for me, amen. What the Father has prepared for me is for me. "Know that a person is not justified by the works of the law, but by faith in Jesus Christ. So, we, too, have put our faith in Christ Jesus that we may be justified by faith in Christ and not by the works of the law, because by the works of the law no one will be justified" (Galatians 2:16, NIV).

If we are always looking for people to support and encourage us before we start doing what God has asked, we may never do what He has asked. Support will not always come. Everyone is not happy with what you are doing, and everyone does not believe in the choices you make, even if you are following the dream and vision for your life. They will not always be the wind underneath you. We have to learn how to encourage ourselves, seek God, and not only follow but believe in what He has called and equipped us to do.

Everyone will not understand, and everyone will not stand in your corner or my corner. It is hard enough to receive this from others in the world, but it is even harder to accept this from your family and friends. Those are the ones you expect to support and encourage you. They do not come through; they do not encourage, and they are not there to uplift and support you. "Therefore, my beloved brethren, be steadfast, immovable, always abounding in the work of the Lord, knowing that your labor is not in vain in the Lord" (1 Corinthians 15:58, NKJV).

Nevertheless, you move forward. You continue forth with what God has placed in your heart to do. In Him, you will find your reward, not in man. What do you do when you have no one in your circle? Where do you turn when everyone is on the outside of the circle questioning why you are still standing in that circle? "My brethren, count it all joy when you fall into various trials, knowing that the testing of your faith produces patience" (James 1:2-3, NKJV).

CHAPTER 8
UNIQUE AND WONDERFUL

"I will praise You, for I am fearfully and wonderfully made; Marvelous are Your works, and that my soul knows very well. My frame was not hidden from You When I was made in secret, and skillfully wrought in the lowest parts of the earth."
(Psalm 139:14-15, NKJV)

Overcoming and Coming Out

I have always loved the story of Ruth. If you have never read it, it is definitely one that you should read with the understanding that it is God who has already written our story. As we are giving to others, even when we are hurting, He sees us, He sees our hearts, and he counts and collects our tears. When we find ourselves stuck in a place of uncertainty and far from what we believe and know to be true, He still loves us. When we feel lost after having lost it all, He still loves and cares for us. He always has our end in sight. Only finding yourself in our one true God will heal, mend, and make you into the whole person made in His image. When we know what the Word of God says about who we are and what He has called us to do, we can rest assured that it will work out for our good and the glory of God. "For we are His workmanship, created in Christ Jesus for good works, which God prepared beforehand that we should walk in them" (Ephesians 2:10, NKJV).

When you begin to study the life of Ruth, you will find out that, instead of this story beginning with Ruth, it will start with the traumatic story of her mother-in-law, Naomi. Both of their lives were turned upside down. No one can put a price on the size of loss and grief for anyone. However, not only did Naomi lose her husband, but she also lost both of her sons, one of whom was married to Ruth.

Since Naomi and both of her daughters-in-law, Orpah and Ruth, were now in a foreign country alone, Naomi told them to leave and go home because she was going to return to her homeland. Naomi was so lost and in a state of grief and believed all of her pain came from God. "...No, my daughters; for it grieves me very much for your sakes that the hand of the Lord has gone out against me" (Ruth 1:13, NKJV).

Naomi attempted to send both daughters-in-law away by telling them to go back to their respective families. However, Ruth refused to leave her side. She was loyal; she was not going to abandon her mother-in-law. She told her she would go where she goes, and she will now consider Naomi's people her people, too. The story then shows Naomi and Ruth's return to Bethlehem.

Just like Naomi and Ruth, we, as women, can often find our lives in disarray. A marriage or relationship ends, a job assignment ends, bankruptcy occurs, and family members pass away. "You keep track of all my sorrows. You have collected all my tears in your bottle. You have recorded each one in your book" (Psalm 56:8, NLT). At times, it can feel as if life is handing us blow after blow. Just like Ruth and Naomi, we, too, feel the sting of devastation and the undeniable hopelessness that tries to overtake us, leaving us defeated and lost. You try to do what you believe is right, yet somehow it appears in the natural that nothing is working.

Ruth, in Bethlehem with Naomi, finds herself gleaning in the fields that belong to Boaz, who is a relative of Naomi. When asked, Ruth asked Boaz to allow her to glean the fields after the reapers have finished. What she does not know is that the owner of the barley field, Boaz, had instructed his workers to leave food in the fields for her to have. He became intrigued with Ruth and instructed Ruth to go to no other field, for her provision was in his field. Just like Ruth, God is our provider and is always looking out for us. We are in position. We will find where our blessing is. It is already waiting for us. "What do you think? If a man has a hundred sheep, and one of them goes astray, does he not leave the ninety-nine and go to the mountains to seek the one that is straying? And if he should find it, assuredly, I say to you, he rejoices more over that sheep than over the ninety-nine that did not go astray. Even so, it is not the will of your Father who is in heaven that one of these little ones should perish" (Matthew 18:12-14, NKJV).

Boaz is Ruth's kinsman-redeemer. A kinsman-redeemer is one that restores. He is also the foreshadowing of Jesus as our Redeemer. He was that for Ruth. Boaz was the life restorer for Ruth. This is exactly what Jesus did for us when He died for our sins and rose again. Our salvation is found only in Him when we just believe, for He is our perfect Redeemer. He is the restorer of our souls, redeeming us back to God when we repent and turn away from sin and accept Jesus and the salvation that He offers as our Savior.

The book shows us that just like Ruth, our beginnings do not determine our end. Ruth ended up having a son, and that son was in the lineage of Jesus. You cannot get much better than that! Looking at our present circumstances by no means tells our completed story. We are redeemed. We are restored. We are a chosen vessel, a royal priesthood, loved and chosen by God. He can make a way. He can restore our way. Only He can bestow our true salvation and peace. "He is the image of the invisible God, the firstborn of all creation. For by Him all things were created, in heaven and on earth, visible and invisible, whether thrones or dominions or rulers or authorities—all things were created through Him and for Him. And He is before all things, and in Him, all things hold together" (Col. 1:15-17, NIV).

Stop and examine your life. What have you been searching for? What has been missing in your life? Is your life in need of a resurrection? If you are not where you desire to be, and if you are not doing what you know you should be doing, begin now to search for the truth. Search for your life, and when you search, know that it can be found in Him. If you are looking for your identity or direction, your instructions have already been prepared for you. They are ready for you, but you have to be willing to follow them.

This is your life! You must seek the Kingdom of God for yourself! In your searching, you will not only find the answers, but you will find real peace, the peace that surpasses all knowledge and perception, bringing you the answers you have been searching for. "Now may the God of the peace who brought up our Lord Jesus from the dead, that great Shepherd of the sheep, through the blood of the everlasting covenant, make you complete in every good work to do His will, working in you what is well-pleasing in His sight, through Jesus Christ, to whom be glory forever and ever. Amen" (Hebrews 13:20-21, NKJV).

CHAPTER 9
GROWING AND LEARNING

"But as for you, you meant evil against me; but God meant it for good, in order to bring it about as it is this day, to save many people alive." (Genesis 50:20, NKJV)

You Are Who He Called You to Be

The life lesson I have learned is not over. Every day, even at my age, I am still learning and discovering more of myself. As we age, the things we once believed about the world, and even about ourselves, can begin to change. We may not be able to change all of the world, but we can change the world that is around us. We can change it by walking in our God-given purpose. The purpose of God is sure to make an impact when we are in place. The impact we are to make is for others, and not necessarily ourselves.

Often, we ask why it had to happen or why it did not happen for me when you see it happening for so many others. Yet, when you begin to compare your life of living and loving God to their life of chasing after and living from the world's point of view, you and me both are absolutely in err. By doing what we are to do, God will be glorified, and we will be blessed as we are a blessing to others. "Now faith is the substance of things hoped for, the evidence of things not seen. For by it the elders obtained a good testimony. By faith, we understand that the worlds were framed by the Word of God so that the things which are seen were not made of things which are visible" (Hebrews 11:1-3, NKJV).

Listen, I have done it! When life gets tough and unexpected things begin to arise, it is not too hard to begin complaining even inwardly, "Is this even fair, Lord? I know I'm doing right. I know I'm praying and obeying and being a blessing when I can, and yet...Lord, are you serious? Do you see what they are doing? Do you see what they said to me and how they have treated me, Lord?" However, in the midst of our incomprehension, we should still be committed to praising Him. Of course, then we need to ask for forgiveness. Our questioning is a lack of faith, and we should not allow it to consume our hearts. If it was not in there, then it would not have come out of our mouth. The Bible says, "Above all else, guard your heart, for everything you do flows from it" (Proverbs 4:23, NIV). Just like you, I'm only human, living in the flesh, doing the best I can to not operate as the world proposes.

Our circumstances can change in a blink of an eye. Things in your life can be lined up. You are focused, you are driven, you are walking and doing all you know you can do. You are trusting God and believing everything is working out for your good. You go to bed, sleeping peacefully, and when you wake up, life happens! Everything can seemingly change in what feels like a blink of an eye. Life happens! What you believed your situation would be, what you had been hoping for, planning for, and working for is all gone.

With everything taking place in the world right now in 2020, every day is a new day, and each day can be drastically different from the day before. Who knew that one virus would not just shut the United States down, but the world as we had grown to know it? On one side, there is the COVID-19 virus circulating through the world, causing havoc and killing the innocent. On the other side, there are injustices that have been taking place for a very long time, in secret, in the dark, that are now being showcased in the light of day. Today is not the same as yesterday, and if we are blessed to see tomorrow, it will not be like today.

The Bible says, "these things I have spoken to you, that in Me you may have peace. In the world you will have tribulation, but be of good cheer, I have overcome the world" (John 16:33, NKJV). Knowing this should calm our hearts, but in some, it never will. It may not automatically make it any easier to bear. Therefore, we must always do our best to stay grounded in the Word of God. We cannot so easily give in to views of the world and those things that are ever available and acceptable by the world but go against the Word. The truth is, Jesus has been more than fair to us all, and we will never be holy and righteous enough to pay back the price that He paid with His blood. He was and is the perfect sacrifice, taking away all of our sins, with His shed blood on the cross.

I Can Do All Things!

Have you ever thought about how it appears that things come easy for other people? No struggle, no strife, no issues. They never lose because they also have the right connections. However, for me, and maybe even for you, it is yet another story of hurt, struggle, and loss at every turn.

As I had previously mentioned, there was a time in my life that I believed I was doing something good. It did not take much for one word of doubt to enter into my head, ultimately making me give up, making me believe that I was not capable of doing anything right and that instead of being a help to others, I would probably end up hurting them. I got scared!

Why did I believe that I could be a nurse? Maybe I should figure out something else to do with my life. I thought this way because I did not even understand if that was the career path that I should be on in the first place. It did not take much for me to doubt myself. When you do not have an understanding of who you are and what you are called to do, it will not take much to throw you off track and back into the water, holding on to the log as your life floats on by.

After the resurrection of Jesus, God instructed the disciples to wait on the promises of God, which was the coming of the Holy Spirit, the Comforter, who held all power. "But the Helper, the Holy Spirit, whom the Father will send in My name, He will teach you all things, and bring to your remembrance all things that I said to you. Peace I leave with you, My peace I give to you; not as the world gives do I give to you. Let not your heart be troubled, neither let it be afraid" (John 14:26-27, NKJV). When you are a child of the Most-High God, and you have accepted and received salvation, you have also been given access to the power of the Holy Spirit. Jesus told us in His word that He would not leave us comfortless. He is always here with us.

Before you can even begin to understand exactly what you should be seeking after for your life, you must understand who you are and that you are capable of doing all things that God has ordained you to do. Every one of us came into this world with a mission, a life purpose. It is up to us to discover what it is, as well as seek the Father and ask for clear direction for your life.

The Word declares, "I can do all things through Christ who strengthens me" (Philippians 4:13, NKJV). We have to believe in our God and in ourselves enough to understand that we do not have to be afraid. Even when things do not work out how we desired them to, we are still capable of doing all He has asked us to accomplish. I believe the issue comes in when we are out of His will and out of place. When we are going after the things of the world, and it is not working out for us, this does not mean that we are a failure. I had to learn and understand this principle. I had to understand that it may not be for me, it may not be the right time, or it just was not the right opportunity. This is what happened to me with desiring to finish my education. There have been times where I believed I was doing the right thing, and even in the right place, yet it appeared that nothing was working or turning out right. "But you shall receive power when the Holy Spirit has come upon you; you shall be witnesses to Me in Jerusalem, and in all Judea and Samaria, and to the end of the earth" (Acts 1:8, NJKV).

Life and death are in the power of the tongue. You are creating your world with the words that come out of your mouth. If you want success, speak success. If you want to achieve all God has already placed in you, begin to believe it, and more importantly, begin to speak it out of your mouth, regardless of what it looks like in the natural.

Do you know what you see does not have to stay the same? It does not have to continue going in the direction that it is traveling. But you have to speak it. You must declare it for it to change. If you do not begin to change what is coming out of your mouth, one thing is for sure: you will continue to have exactly what you declare you will have. Change your thinking, change your belief, and change your words. "The thief does not come except to steal, and to kill, and to destroy. I have come that they may have life and that they may have it more abundantly" (John 10:10, NKJV).

The power of God gives us the ability to make it through, to accomplish all that needs to be accomplished without fear. However, we must remain determined. If it was spoken within our spirit that we will win, then we will win. The key is that we must not give up. We can do it when we put our thoughts in line with what we are speaking out of our mouths and become determined to do our very best. Everything you need is already in you, just as it is already in me. You just got to believe it! Speak life! "Call to Me, and I will answer you, and show you great and [a]mighty things, which you do not know" (Jeremiah 33:3, NKJV).

CHAPTER 10
BEAUTIFUL SAYS I AM

"Strength and honor are her clothing; She shall rejoice in time to come." (Proverbs 31:25, NKJV)

Daughter, You Are Beautiful

When I think about beautiful, the picture of my daughter comes to my mind. She is the epitome of beauty to me because not only is she beautiful on the outside, but she is even more beautiful on the inside. She has a sweet spirit, a calm demeanor, and gives grace to all. This is the same little girl that I spoke of before. The one who had such a strong will that I believed I would never be able to be the strong mother she needed unless the Holy Spirit helped me. Yet looking at her today, no one would ever know or understand her growth and temperance that now swathes her.

Just like she is, and just like I am, we are made and created after the likeness of the Father. "I will praise You, for I am fearfully and wonderfully made; Marvelous are Your works, and that my soul knows very well. My frame was not hidden from You when I was made in secret, and skillfully wrought in the lowest parts of the earth" (Psalm 139:14-15, NKJV).

I do not know if you have ever felt this way or dealt with strong insecurities. The kind of insecurities that you have when other people appear to have all power and confidence about them. After my stint in the hospital and dealing with a serious illness, I started to understand that everyone is not always who they appear to be.

A lot of people do practice that fake-it-until-you-make-it philosophy. I started to realize that every woman that is looking great, walking the walk, and talking the walk is not void of hard and serious issues. I do believe that when I came to understand this, I no longer allowed myself to be intimated by those I saw as in power or control of themselves. "Strength and honor are her clothing; She shall rejoice in time to come" (Proverbs 31:25, NKJV).

Sometimes I could look at someone and ask, "What are you hiding? What is behind that smile on your face and glide in your step?" They are no different than you and me, looking the part on the outside yet struggling on the inside. So, I walk differently now. The confidence I have inside is from the Holy Spirit dwelling within. It is from knowing that God loved me so much that He sent his son to die for me. His shed blood and my acceptance of His unselfish act gave me salvation. How can anyone not be grateful for salvation?

Still, my heart grieves for my parents. I wish I would have cared enough to ask them about their past, about their families. I knew a little, but there is so much more to know and so much more I wonder if I will ever find out. I grieve because of what they did not know to do and who they should have sought out when they were young and in need of God's power in their lives. They did not know how to speak life and the Word into their children. What they knew to do was to do the very best they could. They gave us (their children) the best life we could have, and for that, I will always be grateful. I'm grateful that God gave me to them and them to me.

Even in what the world saw as lacking, God saw as beautiful. God has good thoughts towards His children. Even when we are down and hurt, feeling alone, misunderstood, and discouraged, He has not left us. The Word of God declares that Satan is a liar and hates everything that God loves. Not only does Satan want us all to fail, but he also wants us to hate our lives as much as he hates us and God our Father. "'For I know the thoughts that I think toward you,' says the Lord, 'thoughts of peace and not of evil, to give you a future and a hope'" (Jeremiah 29:11, NKJV). God's love is unfailing, and we must be willing and strong enough to overcome our wrong thinking about ourselves and what we deem as a weakness.

We must begin to forgive ourselves and others so that you and I both can learn to move on with our lives. Unforgiveness will keep you in bondage and delay the needed healing. We are all worthy of love, joy, and peace in our lives. How wonderful is the Word of God as it actively delivers peace and love in time of need?

I pray you will begin to love yourself, and instead of seeking after the world, seek after the one true love who gave you life. Your vision and goals CAN line up with the dreams deep inside of you and turn into the reality you now see in your life. "And you will seek Me and find Me when you search for Me with all your heart" (Jeremiah 29:13, NKJV). As the song goes, "Oh, how I love Jesus because He first loved me." Love lives on!

REFERENCES

· Dictionary by Merriam-Webster: America's most-trusted online dictionary. (n.d.). Retrieved
     August 14, 2020, from https://www.merriam-webster.com/

· Ball of Confusion (That's What the World Is Today), Songwriters: Norman Whitfield / Barrett
     Strong, Sony/ATV Music Publishing LLC

Made in the USA
Middletown, DE
30 September 2021